BEST DAY EVER!

BEST DAY EVER!

A Little Book (by a Little Guy) with
Some Big Ideas on How to Be Happy

by NATHAN GLAD

Foreword by #1 *New York Times* bestselling author
RICHARD PAUL EVANS

ASCENDT PUBLISHING

Best Day Ever! A Little Book (by a Little Guy)
with Some Big Ideas on How to Be Happy
Copyright © 2024 Nathan Glad & Richard Paul Evans

All rights reserved under international and
Pan-American Copyright Conventions.

No part of this book may be reproduced in any form or by any
electronic or mechanical means, including information storage
and retrieval systems, without permission in writing from the publisher,
except by a reviewer, who may quote brief passages in a a review.

Published in 2024 by Ascendt Publishing
a division of Richard Paul Evans Inc.

For purchasing copies of this book in bulk, please contact
Ascendt Publishing at (801) 870-3925

www.NathanGlad.com

Book cover and interior design by
Francine Eden Platt • Eden Graphics, Inc.

Paperback - 978-1-958626-91-7
eBook - 978-1-958626-92-4
Audio - 978-1-958626-93-1

Library of Congress Control Number: 2024935280

Printed and bound in the United States of America

1 2 3 4 5

For my Dad

Best. Day. Ever.

FOREWORD

by Richard Paul Evans

The first time I met Nathan, he was sitting on the front lawn of my assistant's house.

"This is my boss," she said to him. "He's a famous author."

Nathan looked me over for a moment then replied, "Me too."

I loved him immediately. But then, as I soon discovered, so does everyone else. How could you not? In a world screaming victimhood, Nathan chooses resiliency. In a body that dictates so much of what he can and cannot do, Nathan chooses to dictate the meaning and purpose of his life. In a world of dissatisfaction, Nathan chooses gratitude. While people internally debate whether the glass is half empty or half full, Nathan is just grateful for the glass.

Make no mistake, Nathan is fully aware of his circumstance—his estrangement, his limitations, even the danger of his condition. When asked, "What is the most difficult part of an operation? The recovery or the pain?" He replies, "Wondering if I'll wake from it." It's not that he's wearing "rose colored glasses" that are a tint too dark, it's that his attitude is stronger than whatever fate can (and does) throw at him. It's an attitude as fiercely courageous as I've witnessed anywhere. Stronger even than the constant threat of death.

Holocaust survivor and author Viktor E. Frankl said, "The one thing you can't take away from me is the way I choose to respond to what you do to me. The last of one's freedoms is to choose one's attitude in any given circumstance.

Happiness cannot be pursued; it must ensue."

Nathan fully embodies this attitude. Like Frankl, Nathan takes full responsibility for how he views life and how he responds to it.

Ernest Hemingway once wrote, "if I had more time I'd write a shorter book." Do not let the diminutive size of this little book rob you of its profundity. (Of course, that could be said of the author as well.) In its pages, Nathan has left something for all of us if we are courageous enough to accept it. This is his hope, that, though tied to a chair, his thoughts can travel the world and bless lives everywhere. I invite you to help him to that end. God bless and have a happy day.

My sister Courtney and me when we were little.

MEET NATHAN

Hi. My name is Nathan Glad. I'm just like everybody else, except I was born with a condition called Osteogenesis Imperfecta. Most people have trouble remembering those words—sometimes even saying them—so I usually use an easier name: Brittle Bone. Without going into all the medical jargon, what it means is, my bones are weak. In fact, they have the consistency of a pretzel. And I like pretzels. Just not for bones.

But Brittle Bone isn't the most important part of me. Not even close. It's just what people notice about me first. So here's the important stuff:

I have two siblings and a great mother and father. (Though something about that changed recently. I'll get to that later.)

I can write with both hands, since I had to learn to write with whichever hand wasn't broken at the time.

My initials are **N.R.G.** (Nathan Ryan Glad), and if you say it fast, it sounds like ENERGY, which my mom says I have a lot of.

I sleep with my eyes open. (I know, that probably sounds a little creepy.)

I love collecting Legos, and I attend high school like any other guy my age—which as of right now is seventeen.

I'm pretty good with numbers so I want to be an accountant. I get good grades, and there's nothing wrong with my brain.

There's one other very important thing you should know about me. I'm happy. Very happy. Life is good. Always!

I'm hardly ever unhappy. I mean I have my moments like everyone else, but not often. You could say that every day is the best day of my life. That's kind of my catchphrase, which is why we named this book what we did: Every day's the ***Best Day Ever!*** You may not believe me, but it's true. You can ask anyone who knows me.

But I also know that my life doesn't have to be happy. If I wanted, I could find some pretty convincing reasons to be *un*happy. But I don't want to. The important thing is, I've learned that *I have a say in the matter*. And there's things I do to keep happy. I think I will call them "happiness hacks." And they've worked for me. Especially during the hard times. And there have been a few hard times. If you give them a shot, I think they'll work for you too.

I know this is a little book. I'm little too, but size doesn't always matter. Like my mom says, good things often come in small packages. I don't think that a book on "how to be happy" should be a thousand pages long. Or even a hundred. Being happy shouldn't take a manual. It shouldn't be complicated or require genius. If that was the case, then the higher your IQ the happier you would be, right? We know that's not always the case. Or maybe even the norm.

All these ideas on happiness are things that have helped me in my life. I thought it would be a good idea to add some note pages in the back so you could write down your own thoughts and ideas on happiness. Though my ideas are simple, some might not seem so simple to do in real life. But I do them—and my life is real. I know you can do it too. If I can, you can.

Here are my seven *Happiness Hacks*. I'll explain them as we go. I hope you're ready.

My 7 Happiness Hacks™

- Choose happiness
- Sharpen your sense of humor
- Take the hard times day by day
- Don't pay attention to what others think
- Find your superpower
- Celebrate small victories
- Be grateful for today

CHOOSE HAPPINESS

Sometimes people ask me, why are you so happy? Sometimes they say it like being happy was a crime or something. Or maybe they just think that with the way my life, or my body is, I *shouldn't* be happy. Of course, like you, I have reasons *not* to be happy. Everyone has hard things in their lives. I could, if I wanted to, make a list of things I have to be unhappy about. I don't want to, but, if I did, this might be what that list would look like. (It's not in any particular order.)

Reason number 1 to be unhappy:

I don't know how long I'll live. They say that I've already beaten all the odds. In fact, on the day I was born, my grandparents were out planning my funeral. That's what the doctors told them to do. No one (except my parents) thought I would survive birth. I was born with more than 30 broken bones, which thankfully I don't remember, but I lived. And I'm pretty happy about that.

People say the funniest things to me. The other day a man walked up to me and said, "You know, you're lucky to be alive." I looked up at him and said, "So are you."

I don't know, I guess to him I didn't look like I should be alive. But, for now, I am alive, and I'm grateful for that. My last name is **Glad**. I think it's a pretty appropriate last name for me.

Reason number 2 to be unhappy:

Every day I miss my father. Shortly after I started this book, my father died. He was my best friend. We even had a special backpack he carried me in. He took me all sorts of places, like car shows (I love those. I even got to be a judge once.), hiking, plays and movies, you name it.

Being carried by my dad

At Christmastime, when he carried me around, I felt a little bit like Tiny Tim and his father, Bob Cratchit at the end of *A Christmas Carol* movie when Mr. Cratchit holds tiny Tim on his shoulder and Tim says, "God Bless Us, Everyone."

My father wanted me to have the same experiences and opportunities that other children have. Even though I miss him terribly, I know he wouldn't want me to be unhappy. I know he would tell me that. He was smart that way.

Reason number 3 to be unhappy:

I have a lot of pain. Do you know that scene in the *X-Men* when Rogue asks Wolverine if it hurts when his claws come out, and he says, "Every time." That's what it's like for me. Only it's not cool claws, it's broken bones. My mother and I have lost count of how many bones I've broken. And yes, it hurts every time I break a bone, just like it would hurt you to break a bone. If you've broken a bone, you know what I'm talking about. If you haven't, well, you'll just have to trust me. Breaking bones is not something you want to do or will ever get used to.

Reason number 4 to be unhappy:

I will never have a "normal" life. I will always need someone to take care of me.

Playing T-ball

I can't run. I can't even walk. (Heck, I can't even stand.) I can't play sports. (That's not completely true. There's a cool charity that helps kids like me with disabilities that let me play T-ball in my wheelchair.)

If you want to get really personal, I can't even go to the bathroom by myself. I'm a teenager now. You don't think that's embarrassing?

Reason number 5 to be unhappy:

I don't look like other people, which is why, growing up, other kids made fun of me. My mother used to push me in my wheelchair to school. A group of kids were always outside the school. When they saw me, they'd call me names. They said I was weird looking, and I looked like an alien. I don't think I'm weird looking. I just look like me.

Also, people think I'm much younger than I am. One time, I was at a McDonalds, and a little boy was running around me. His mother said,

"Don't run around like that. You might hurt the baby." I looked at her and said, "I'm not a baby!" You should have seen her face.

. . . AND THAT'S MY SHORT LIST

That's my short list of reasons to be unhappy. I think it's a pretty convincing one. Maybe it's as good (or bad) as yours. But this isn't a competition. I could make a longer one if I wanted to, but I don't want to. Besides, you get the point.

Until now, I've never made a list like that. I see no reason to. Why? Because it doesn't make me happy. And I've decided that I *want* to be happy. And, properly used, *want* is a powerful thing. *Want* is usually the beginning of any change in your life.

You can make a list of things to be unhappy about too. Many, many people do. If not on paper, then in their minds. They make lists and go through them, over and over, reminding themselves about how much they have to be unhappy about and how unfair their life is. And guess what, (no surprise) they are unhappy!

> *Comparing your life to others isn't smart.*
> —Gladitude

One of the things these unhappy people do to build their unhappiness list is to compare their life with other people's lives. I think some of the most painful things we can do is to compare our lives to others. These people look at someone else and say, "They have something I don't, so it's not fair and I'm unhappy." Or, "How come they have more money than me? or better clothes? or how come good things happen to them and not me?"

I think that thinking that way is tragic. And, it's not a very honest thing to do either. Firstly, we don't even know all the hard things other people have in their lives. Some people look like everything is going great for them when they're usually not. It's like dressing up in beautiful clothes when you feel ugly underneath. It happens all the time.

Secondly, we're kind of cherry picking. We look at something someone has, but we only pick out the one thing, without looking at what they don't have. Like I said, it's not honest.

> *Unhappiness is **boring.***
> – Nathan's Gladitude

I find that a lot of people, even some who are older and smarter than me, don't know that happiness is a choice. But it is. And if you're one of the smart ones who wants to be happy, I congratulate you.

Someone once asked me, "Are you a glass half full or glass half empty kind of guy?"

I thought about it then said, "I'm just happy to have a glass."

That glass is my life, and I try to fill it each day with as much happiness as possible.

So let's do something that *will* lead to happiness. Let's create a happiness list. It's a great exercise. Here is mine so far:

Nathan's Happy List

(Why I'm happy or things that make me happy)

1. I am alive
2. I have a wonderful family
3. I have a mom
4. I have a dad
5. I have a brother
6. I have a sister
7. I have a dog
8. My home
9. My bed
10. Seatbelts

11. Donuts
12. Video games
13. Games
14. Camps
15. Hot dogs
16. BBQ ribs
17. Ice Cream
18. I have a large Lego collection
19. I have a few good friends
20. Making homemade root beer
21. Puppets
22. Movies
23. Stuffed bears
24. Chocolate
25. Vacations
26. Wheelchairs
27. Doctors
28. Bandages
29. Teddy bears

30. Blankets
31. Pillows
32. Heat
33. Soup
34. Cars
35. Airplanes
36. Elevators
37. Smooth sidewalks
38. Food
39. Water
40. Garlic mashed potatoes
41. Digging holes at the beach
42. Iron Man
43. Disneyland & Disney World
44. Birthdays
45. Funny videos
46. School
47. Drawing

48. Coloring
49. Money (who doesn't like money?)
50. Hats
51. Memories
52. A good joke
53. A smile
54. Pizza
55. Transformers
56. Audiobooks
57. Straight A's
58. Someone who will hold the door
59. Pictures with friends
60. Keychains (I collect them)
61. Grandma's cookies (especially chocolate chip)
62. Fuzzy socks
63. Mac and Cheese
64. Fun P.J.'s
65. A sunny day

66. Fluffy clouds
67. Baseball
68. My long eyelashes
69. Paved hiking trails
70. A fresh haircut
71. Long bendy stairs
72. Conversation in movie quotes
73. A good night sleep
74. The table in my bathroom
75. Going through the car wash
76. Clean eyeglasses
77. Church
78. Seminary
79. Health
80. A do nothing day
81. New clothes
82. Christmas
83. Flowers
84. The smell of rain

85. *Psych* (TV series)
86. *Monk* (TV series)
87. T.V. Shows
88. Wipes (for face, hands and hindquarters)
89. Bread
90. Hot buttered rolls
91. No homework
92. Puppy love
93. Laughing
94. Cleared sidewalks
95. Switch games
96. Car seats
97. Web slingers
98. Book writing with an awesome author 😁
99. Spell check/autocorrect
100. Writing this list

And that's just the beginning. If you've never made a list like this, try it. Just doing it will make you happy.

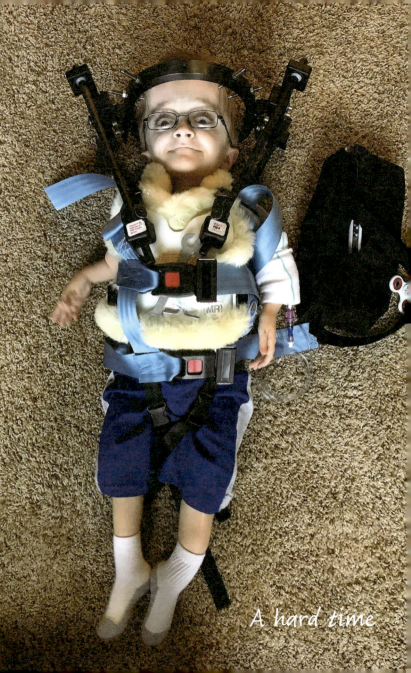

TAKE THE HARD TIMES ONE DAY AT A TIME

The thing about my condition is that it's always facing a new challenge. As my organs grow, they put pressure on my bones. As my head grows, it puts more pressure on my neck. This is something that is very dangerous. If my neck bones can't hold up my head, then it's going to sink down to my spine. This is what happened to me. And it started pinching my spinal cord at the base of my skull. If it got any worse, it could paralyze everything below my neck and I would be a quadriplegic. In the worst scenario, I would no longer be able to breath.

My doctor recommended a neck fusion to stop my head from sinking any lower on my spine. To do this, they would take bone from my ribs and pack it around my vertebrae. They would have to place rods from my skull down my spine. This meant I would lose all mobility in my neck. Forever. But I'd rather not be able to turn my head then lose all feeling and ability below my neck.

The biggest question the doctors had was if the rods in my bones would hold, because, like I said, my bones are really, really fragile. I was also told that it would be very, very painful.

I was in the doctor's office and had just been told that I needed a second surgery, and I would be placed in a halo. My father asked me if I was worried about the operation. I said, "No."

He asked, "Why not?"

I said, "I can't change what needs to happen and being sad doesn't make it better, so I am going to be happy."

My dad just smiled and shook his head. I'm simply not a worrier. In fact, it wasn't even my idea to put this in the book because I hardly think about it. But I'm told that most people worry. Maybe you do. I think that often the most pain we feel isn't because of what actually happens to us, but because we are thinking about what *might* happen to us. If you have a good imagination, you can really think of a lot of frightening things that can happen.

Worrying can double or triple the time we are in pain, because worrying *is* painful. And, listen to me, *you can't worry and be happy at the same time*. It just doesn't work. It's like swallowing with your mouth open. You can't do it. At least I can't. (My brother Jason says he can.)

The Bible says, *sufficient to the day is the evil thereof*. That means that there's enough bad things happening in each day to make it worse by imagining what bad thing *might* happen tomorrow. I think that's pretty wise. Why should we worry about things that might not happen. In fact, why worry about things that will happen? It's like experiencing the bad thing twice.

I think worrying is a habit. A bad one. Like biting your fingernails or always being late to things. And, like both of those things, it's a habit we can change. Sometimes we can change just by looking it in the eyes, or ourselves in the eyes, and say, "What good is coming from me worrying about this? Is it making me happy?

(Trust me, it's not.) Is it making me safer? Probably not."

That doesn't mean you can't think about the possibility of bad things and, when possible, prepare for them. In fact, that's pretty wise. But preparing and worrying aren't the same thing. As someone once said, "Worrying is as effective as trying to solve a math problem by chewing bubble gum."

Another reason not to worry

I've read that your physical body can't tell the difference between real and imaginary things—which is why your heart beats fast during a scary movie or a bad dream—so when you imagine something horrible happening, your body reacts like it really did, which can't be good. Maybe that's why we have the saying, "She worried herself sick."

We should deal with our battles, each day, just as they come to us.

Easy does it. Take life as it comes.

CULTIVATE YOUR SENSE OF HUMOR

I used to run a dating service for chickens, but I had trouble making hens meet.

Someone stole my mood ring. I don't know how I feel about that.

I broke my finger last week. On the other hand, I'm okay. (very applicable, right?)

I took the shell off my snail to see if he'd go faster. He didn't. It made him sluggish.

You don't need a parachute to go skydiving. You just need one to go skydiving twice.

I told my mother she was drawing her eyebrows too high. She looked surprised.

I ordered a chicken and an egg from Amazon. I'll let you know which comes first.

Here's a horrible one:

What do you call a dog with no legs? It doesn't matter, it's not going to come anyway.

Sorry for that last one, but I love jokes. I love to hear them and tell them. I once broke a bone laughing, and it wasn't even my funny bone. (It was a rib, of course.)

I love to laugh. They say that laughter is the best medicine, and it really is. And, considering my medical history, I should know.

Once, a few days before my surgery, one of my doctors (my neurosurgeon) and me got into a joke contest. He asked me, "How many apples a day does it take to keep the doctor away?"

I said, "I don't know."

He said, "It depends on your aim."

I'm always a little nervous before a surgery. Sometimes I wonder if I'll wake up after one. But I'm still not unhappy. Telling jokes with that doctor helped. That's the power of humor. Mark Twain wrote: "Humor is mankind's greatest blessing. Against the assault of laughter, nothing can stand."

> *I think that laughter is the sound of happiness.*
> — Gladitude

Humor is magical. It can create happiness out of thin air. It can strengthen relationships and even make friends. It can calm tense situations.

I say *cultivate* a sense of humor because that is what we need to do. "Cultivate" means to promote the growth of something. Just like you can cultivate a singing voice, or skill, you can cultivate humor. Here are a couple tips to cultivating a sense of humor.

Memorize a few good jokes to share wherever you go.

Don't take yourself too seriously. The graveyards are full of really important people with important places to go.

Speaking of graveyards. A woman stands up at a funeral and says, "I'd like to say a word."
The preacher says, "Go ahead."
She says, "Plethora," then sits down.
The preacher says, "Thank you. That means a lot."

That's all I have to say about that.

HUMOR IS MANKIND'S GREATEST BLESSING. AGAINST THE ASSAULT OF LAUGHTER NOTHING CAN STAND.

MARK TWAIN

DON'T PAY ATTENTION TO WHAT OTHERS THINK

Worrying about what others think is a big waste of time. It's also a surefire way to be unhappy. The worst part is, it gives someone else control over your emotions, which means they have control over you. Like a puppet. I know that this might seem hard or even impossible to do, but it's really not.

I'm glad I learned this one early on. One time I was at a church, and there were some children pointing at me and laughing. I could hear some of the things they were saying. They weren't very nice. My mother was furious. As we left the church, she said to me, "You heard those children. Why aren't you angry like I am." I said, "Why should I? They don't know me."

> *Worrying about what others think is a waste of time.*
> — Gladitude

I think the reason we are hurt by what people say, isn't because of what they say, but because of what we *think* about what they say. I believe this for two reasons.

1. If someone says something mean about us, but we don't hear it, it doesn't hurt us, right? Or if they say it in a language we don't understand, we don't feel bad either. So this means that it has to go through our ears and then our brain for

us to give it validation to turn it into something that hurts us.

2. If someone called you a giraffe, would it hurt your feelings? No. Because you know you're not a giraffe. The problem is when they say something mean and we think, *maybe they're right*, or *maybe it's true*. That means we are validating what they say. Holding onto things is also a way of validating what someone says.

Another powerful way to handle people who say mean things is to forgive them immediately. Sometimes people think forgiving someone is "letting them off the hook" or giving them a gift they don't deserve. But it really has little to do with them. Forgiveness is a choice we make to not hold onto things people do or say.

I mean, maybe someone was having a bad day. Should you join them in their bad day?

If you do, you're in trouble, because there's always someone having a bad day.

One time a friend of mine was talking to a woman at a shipping company. She was angry and mean and kept telling him that she couldn't help him. Instead of getting angry, he paused for a moment and asked, "Are you okay?"

The woman hesitated then said, "What do you mean?"

He said, "You sound upset. I just wanted to make sure you were okay."

She was quiet for a moment then said, "I'm sorry. It's just been kind of a hard day. I didn't mean to take it out on you." Then she cheerfully helped him get the things shipped to him.

THE REASON WE ARE HURT BY WHAT PEOPLE SAY ISN'T BECAUSE OF WHAT THEY SAY, BUT BECAUSE OF WHAT WE THINK ABOUT WHAT THEY SAY.

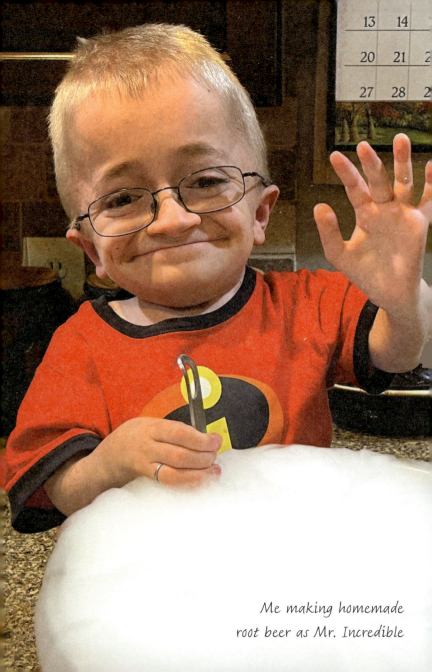

Me making homemade root beer as Mr. Incredible

FIND YOUR SUPERPOWER
(Then use it to save the world!)

There are two things I really love (besides my family and Culvers fried cheese curds). They are Legos and Superheroes. I love watching movies with people with superpowers. Or, better yet, people who make their own superpowers like Batman and, my favorite, Iron Man.

I believe, and I've thought a lot about this, that everyone has a superpower. I'm not saying they can bend steel or see through walls or anything like that. But actually, much more practical powers. I may not look like it, but I have superpowers too. And it's not breaking bones—even though I'm pretty good at that. It took me a few years to discover what it was. But it is a very special superpower. One that can change the world. Do you want to know what it is?

I attract people.

There it is. It's true. I don't know why I have this superpower, but I do. *Especially* at Costco, I'm a magnet for old ladies. They always come up to me and start talking. (And then they cry. It's actually pretty weird.)

Everywhere I go, people want to meet me. If my mom takes me to get a hamburger, people at other tables will come talk to me.

I realized that I could do some good with this. But it's not just realizing that we have a superpower—we need to use it for good!

Imagine if Superman, or Spider man had all that power but just sat around playing video games all day. What point would their superpower be?

I've discovered that I find happiness using my superpower to bring happiness to others.

With my power to attract, I started a hot dog stand to raise money for people in need.

This is my mom and me cutting the ribbon on my hot dog stand.

I wrote a book (before this one). It was a children's book called *Climbing with Tigers*. It was about a little black bird named Blue. A play producer found it and decided to make a play from it. A lot of people came to see it. Personally, I watched it 22 times. I'm not exaggerating. I would have watched it more if I didn't have school or homework.

One time, I was at a baseball game, and a group of teenage girls surrounded me. My father said, "Look at all the pretty, young women you attract."

I said, "It doesn't do me any good."

And when I posted on social media that I was going to write this book on happiness, thousands of people showed their support long before I was even done. In fact, I had more than 30,000 Tik Tok followers! I'm grateful for my superpower, and I'm committed to use it for good.

My author friend, Richard Paul Evans, once asked a group of children at a middle school to share their superpower. One kid raised his hand. Even though he was younger than me, he was much larger. He looked really strong too. Like a miniature version of the Incredible Hulk. He walked up to the microphone to tell us what his superpower was. I thought he was going to say, "I can beat people up," or "I can tip over cars." Instead, he said,

"I can make babies laugh."

He certainly made everyone laugh. What a great superpower. He's going to be a great dad someday.

CELEBRATE VICTORIES

I'm pretty sure that I'll never win a gold medal in any sport or climb Mount Everest, but I've climbed some of my own mountains. And I don't need to compare my challenges to anyone else's. Here are a few of them.

MOUNTAIN ONE

At the age of six, I became frustrated at my inability to walk. So, after a lot of practice, I learned to get myself around the house by what my family calls, "Bum Scooting." I got pretty good at it, and it brought me, and my parents, a lot of freedom. I celebrated my freedom by scooting myself wherever I wanted to go.

MOUNTAIN TWO

At one hard time in my life, I had broken bones in both of my arms. One of my arms never really reconnected to my shoulder, which means I can flap it around like a wing. You can literally bend my arm behind my back. During this time, there were a lot of things I couldn't do. One of those things was writing.

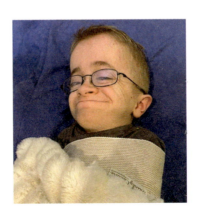

Being able to write is important to me, and I wasn't willing to accept the inability to write. It took a lot of effort, but I taught myself to write again. I had to do this multiple times when I broke my right arm, also when I became partially paralyzed after one of my surgeries. I celebrate this by drawing pictures, something my father liked to do as well.

MOUNTAIN THREE

When I first started going to school, I was put in a "resource class" because of all the school I'd missed due to my medical procedures. I wanted to be in a regular class, so I took all my schoolwork seriously and worked as hard as I could. Now I'm taking Honor Classes, including Sophomore Honors English. I'm also taking college courses.

I refuse to accept any grade less than an "A" and I always ask my teachers for extra work so I can learn more and get better grades. My parents and teachers are proud of me, which, if you think about it, is kind of a celebration in itself.

Why stop celebrating at just victories? We can celebrate anything we go through. Every time I broke a bone, my parents would get us chocolate donuts. It always gave me something to look forward to after going through something awful.

A victory could be conquering anything difficult, even getting out of bed in the morning when you don't feel like it. Or being nice to someone when they've been less than nice to you. Anything you do out of the ordinary can be celebrated. And celebrating lifts your spirits.

So do like that old song says, "Celebrate good times! Come on!"

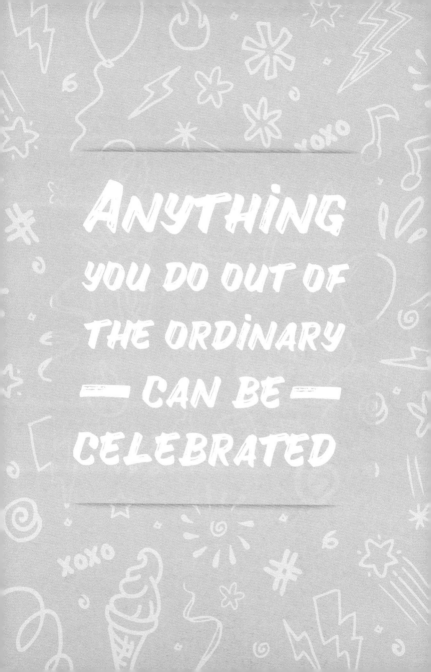

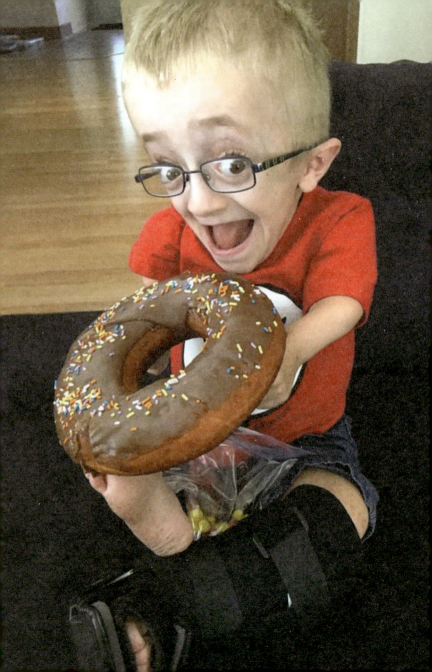

TODAY IS THE BEST DAY EVER

Be grateful for what you have today

I saved this final *Happiness Hack* for last because I think it's the most important.

I have a favorite saying: *Every day is the best day ever!* I say it every day. I really do. And I believe it. Even if it's a hard day, it still is the best day because what I learn from the bad days makes me a better and stronger person.

Sometimes I feel like I was born with this. (Maybe gratitude is my second superpower!)

I'm told that my first words weren't Mama or Papa, like most children, but "Thank You." (Actually, "Gank You." I was too young to make the TH sound.)

If you're trying to create happiness in your life, take a lesson from dogs. To them, every day is a new gift, and every sunrise is a new opportunity. Life is a gift. Being grateful for a gift is not only a big deal, but appropriate. And, if you want to be happy, gratitude is super important. How important? Well, I don't think you can be grateful and *un*happy at the same time. Or *un*grateful and happy at the same time. Either way, it can't happen. It's like I said before, it's like swallowing with your mouth open. It doesn't work.

To take this one step further, I don't think that people are grateful because they're happy. I think they're happy because they're grateful.

The thing about gratitude is that it is scientifically proven to be a skill we can grow. And, as my grandmother who teaches piano says, "Practice makes perfect." Well, I'm not perfect at gratitude, but I'm getting pretty good at it. When I think about all the kindnesses shown me, it fills my heart with incredible happiness. See, they're kind of the same thing.

How do we develop gratitude? It's all about awareness. Remember that awful list I made at the beginning of this book: everything I had to be unhappy about? Well, if you haven't done it already, get started on making your list on *everything you have to be happy about*. That should be a very, very long list.

If you're looking for gratitude, just grab a notebook and pen and start looking around you. There are things to be grateful for everywhere. If you can read this book, be grateful that you can read! Or, better yet, that you can see! Every day that you wake without pain, shout out in gratitude. If you can walk, you should jump in the air right now with gratitude. If you have someone to love, you are super, super lucky. If someone loves you back, well, a hundred times that.

How do you develop gratitude? First, get good at finding things to be grateful for, then get even better at showing it. I tell you, it will only make things better in your life.

If you have friends, let them know how grateful you are to have them. And they will be even better friends.

If you're a business person, tell your customers how grateful you are for their business. They'll bring you more.

I know some people whose superpower is gratitude, and they have incredible lives. Like me.

EPILOGUE

That's it. My seven happiness hacks. I hope you found them helpful. Why is it important to be happy right now? Well, like I said in the beginning, there is no guarantee on how long I will live. But, if you think about it, I'm really no different than you. There's no guarantee for any of us. Just like my dad. One morning he said "Goodbye, I love you" then went out the front door with my brother on a simple hiking trip. I never saw him again. 😞

This reminds me that all life is fragile, not just mine, so what do you want that precious time you have to be filled with? Sadness, despair, self-pity? Or joy, gratitude, and happiness? It's up to you. But, for me, I think happiness is a pretty smart choice. In fact, it makes me happy just thinking about it.

Thank you for reading my book. I wish you a very happy life and a happy day. In fact, I wish you your best day ever.

ABOUT THE AUTHOR

Nathan Ryan Glad was not supposed to survive birth. He was born in Salt Lake City, Utah with a condition called Osteogensis Imperfecta (OI), more commonly known as brittle bone disease. Nathan has the most severe form of OI of anyone living today.

Despite the daunting challenges Nathan faces daily, he chooses to be happy every day of his life. His personal motto is the inspiration for this book's title: "Every day is the best day ever."

In August of 2023, Nathan met with best-selling author Richard Paul Evans to discuss the writing and publishing of this book—something Evans passionately encouraged.

Nathan currently lives in Taylorsville, Utah with his mother and two siblings.

Join the NATHAN GLAD HAPPINESS PROJECT

Help me share happiness around the world!

1. Tell someone a joke!

2. Share my book with a lot of people. I mean, really a lot. (My publisher has a discounted "share" bundle and a super discounted "Mission" bundle).

3. Go to NathanGlad.com and sign up for my mailing list. (I'll send you a weekly happiness quote. I'll also let you know when our **Best Day Ever** and **Be Glad** T-shirts are ready!)

My Happiness List